BOOK ANALYSIS

Written by Benjamin Taylor

The Constant Gardener

BY JOHN LE CARRÉ

Bright
≡Summaries.com

JOHN LE CARRÉ

ENGLISH NOVELIST

- **Born in Dorset (England) in 1931.**
- **Notable works:**
  - *The Spy Who Came in from the Cold* (1963), novel
  - *Tinker Tailor Soldier Spy* (1974), novel
  - *The Night Manager* (1993), novel

John le Carré, born in Dorset, England in 1931 as David Cornwell, is an internationally renowned writer of espionage novels and short stories. After studying at the University of Oxford and enjoying a brief teaching career, le Carré was employed by the British Foreign Service in West Berlin, where he learnt many of the informed details about espionage and international relations that are found throughout his works. While working for MI5 and MI6, le Carré began writing, and launched a career as a novelist spanning over 50 years and dozens of books with his first work, *Call for the Dead* (1961). His first successful novel was *The Spy Who Came in from the Cold* (1963), which was an internationally acclaimed bestseller. His espionage novels are often set during the Cold War and feature British intelligence agents in a more bureaucratic and realistic light, compared with the traditional glamorisation of spies in popular fiction. Many of his books and stories have been successfully adapted for the cinema and television, and he is now one of the most well-respected and celebrated English novelists of the postwar period.

THE CONSTANT GARDENER

CORRUPTION IN KENYA

- **Genre:** novel
- **Reference edition:** Le Carré, J. (2006) *The Constant Gardener*. London: Sceptre.
- **1st edition:** 2001
- **Themes:** scandal, Africa, AIDS, Britain, corruption, grief, diplomacy, murder

The Constant Gardener, published in 2001, is John le Carré's 18th novel, and represents another step in his move away from the Cold War as his primary subject matter and into broader and more complex contemporary issues. It details a pharmaceutical corruption scandal in Kenya and damaging Western influence in Africa, and is reportedly loosely based on a real-life scandal in Kano, Nigeria. As is typical of le Carré's work, it picks up on the undercurrents of shady governmental and corporate dealings and their effects on the world's geo-political climate. He makes it known that, during the course of his research for the book, he found that the truth of the Western exploitation of Africa is far worse than his fictionalised version. The novel was a critical and commercial success and was adapted into a film in 2005, starring Ralph Fiennes and Rachel Weisz.

SUMMARY

A MURDER IN KENYA

In Nairobi, Kenya, Sandy Woodrow, a senior British diplomat, hears that Tessa Quayle has been found dead in a sealed overturned car along with her decapitated driver. She was said to be travelling with the Belgian doctor Arnold Bluhm, who is missing. Woodrow informs her husband, Justin Quayle, another diplomat and friend, and they go and identify the body. Justin goes to live with Woodrow and his wife Gloria while the furore surrounding the murders dies down. They go back to Justin's house to recover some documents, and Woodrow recalls a time when he refused to entertain documents Tessa produced for him incriminating the corrupt Moi government in Kenya. He remembers also having sent her a letter declaring his love for her the same night.

Justin becomes increasingly introverted, keeping tight hold of the bag he fetched from his house. The press is becoming wildly accusatory, and it is rumoured that Tessa was having an affair with Bluhm and was even carrying his child before her death. Woodrow speaks to his superior at the High Commission, who warns him not to reveal too much to anyone about Tessa, implying that they are hiding something about her. Woodrow remembers visiting her in hospital soon after she gave birth to a stillborn child. Bluhm was there, as well as a woman dying next to her. Delirious from her grief and the after-effects of childbirth, Tessa claimed that the woman had been killed by men in white suits – a claim which Woodrow dismissed. Back in the present, police come to question Woodrow, and ask him alarmingly detailed questions about Tessa. He remembers having met Tessa again, when she gave him an envelope of documents purportedly revealing a major corruption scandal, though Woodrow refused to act upon it.

INVESTIGATIONS

Following Tessa's funeral, Justin leaves Kenya for England. On the plane he recalls his own conversations with the police, during which he revealed the nature of his marriage and what happened to Tessa following her miscarriage. He too was asked about the dying woman, named Wanza, whose death he associated with the ThreeBees company, a large British concern in Kenya that, among many other things, sold pharmaceutical products. They asked him about a man named Lorbeer, though he feigned ignorance. They asked him further questions relating to Tessa's connection to ThreeBees, claiming that she and Arnold Bluhm assailed the company with warnings, letters and threats for months before her death. They claimed that one of her letters contained details of a new pharmaceutical drug used to treat tuberculosis which had dangerous side effects. For some reason, Justin was very evasive about certain details and refused to tell them which documents he took from the house.

In London, Justin goes to the Foreign Office, and amongst condolences is asked to provide any documents or the laptop belonging to Tessa that he might have. It is revealed that Bluhm is being blamed for Tessa's death, though Justin is incre-dulous. Soon after, he is approached by the two policemen tasked with questioning him in Kenya, who tell him that he is being tracked by the Foreign

Office and that he should leave the country to lose them. He does so, and holes up in an Italian villa owned by Tessa's now-dead family to read all the information he recovered from her office.

NEW FACTS EMERGE

He finds out about her escalating investigations relating to ThreeBees, its CEO Kenneth K. Curtiss and a drug called Dypraxa, which is manufactured by a Swiss company called Karol Vita Hudson (KVH), and which ThreeBees has been selling without proper safety checks or dosages to huge numbers of people in Africa, employing Lorbeer to do so. Transcriptions of police reports provided to Justin show ThreeBees officials being evasive when asked about Tessa and her reported contact with them. Justin manages to gain access to Tessa's laptop and, amongst other things, finds out that Arnold Bluhm is a homosexual, proving the claims of Tessa's infidelity false. However, the laptop is wiped clean by a virus before he can access her emails.

Back in Kenya, Woodrow, as acting head of the High Commission, lies to the staff at the British Consulate, telling them that Bluhm is being blamed for Tessa's murder, and painting Justin to be a grief-stricken, mad conspiracy theorist. Justin goes to Germany to talk to a woman named Birgit, a correspondent of Tessa's who tells him about a letter she received from Lorbeer, confessing everything about the problems with Dypraxa and its use in Africa despite this. She tells him about a woman, Lara Emrich, who helped develop the drug but attempted unsuccessfully to bring to light its problems, and whose career has been ruined as a result. When he returns to his hotel, Justin is beaten and gagged by an unknown group of assailants who tell him to go back to England and keep his nose out.

Following his beating, Justin tracks down Lara Emrich in America and asks her about the details of Dypraxa. She tells him that the drug was released without proper tests in order to maximise profit, that African people were being used as guinea pigs to test the drugs for foreign markets, and that the scientific community was being pressured to produce favourable but false research about the drug. She gives Justin Lobeer's address in Kenya, and he makes a lucky escape from his tails.

Donahue, a senior British spy, has a meeting with Kenneth K. Curtiss, who screams at him to stop Justin's investigations and back him up in the British government. Investors have been deserting him all day due to the growing scandal surrounding Dypraxa, and one of his close aides takes Donahue aside and offers him the story of what happened to Bluhm and Tessa in exchange for money.

RETRACING STEPS

Back in Kenya, Justin travels to an aid camp called Loki – the same journey that Tessa and Bluhm had taken months before – to confront Lorbeer. He poses as a journalist for *The Times* and interviews Lorbeer about the work they do there. Lorbeer is fiercely critical of big business' manipulation of Africa for profit. Justin reveals his identity to Lorbeer and accuses him of his own role in the manipulation of African tragedy. Tessa and Bluhm had come for the same purpose and recorded a long confession from Lorbeer – who then betrayed them and had them killed.

In the final chapter of the novel, Justin returns to the scene of Tessa's death, and it is revealed that he too suffers her fate – betrayed again by Lorbeer, he is beaten and killed. However, he manages to send off the information he gathered to Tessa's lawyers and, though the information is dismissed by the British government, it slowly starts to generate traction.

CHARACTER STUDY

JUSTIN QUAYLE

Justin Quayle, the protagonist of the novel, is an English diplomat living and working in Kenya as a representative of the British government. He is middle-aged and described as having a "studiously handsome face and greying black hair" (p. 27), and is renowned for his love of gardening and knowledge of horticulture. He comes from a privileged background, having gone to Eton and his father similarly having been a part of the British Foreign Office, which eased "his path into the 'family firm', which was what his father called the Foreign Office" (p. 145). He worked in Bosnia during the Bosnian War (1992-95), and on returning home to England, he met Tessa, his much younger wife, while in Cambridge. The novel starts with his being told of Tessa's death, and he is increasingly overwhelmed by this loss, spending the rest of the novel, and indeed his life, attempting to understand what had happened to her: "There was the inescapable suggestion that a good deal of the Justin they knew, and perhaps all of it, was going with her to the hereafter" (p. 118).

Justin is increasingly defined in contrast to Tessa, in terms of both his nature and the way that it affects his actions: "He was objective, she was emotional. He played the safe centre, she worked the dangerous edges" (p. 87). Though a kind, moral and wholly gentle man throughout the book, he is representative of the placidity of the British Foreign Office in Africa, with the image of the classic 'English Gentleman' (p. 62) – with an "old Etonian smile" and absolute loyalty to the interests of the Crown. We find that as he goes on his journey of rediscovering Tessa's secrets, and the nature of the scandal she uncovered, he becomes less reserved and more committed to discovering the truth despite the potentially disastrous results of its indictment of British actions abroad. *The Constant Gardener* details Justin's retracing of Tessa's investigations, and he does this to the end, when he is betrayed by Lorbeer, beaten and killed in the same spot as her as a result of his discoveries.

TESSA QUAYLE

Though she is never alive in the novel, having been killed at the start as a result of her investigations into the corrupt and damaging work of the Swiss pharmaceutical company Karol Vita Hudson, Tessa Quayle's presence and actions hang over *The Constant Gardener*. She is in her early twenties, a trained lawyer and from a very wealthy background which fundamentally affects the nature of her character: "she was born rich but that never impressed her. She had no interest in money. She needed far less of it than the aspiring classes. But she knew that she had no excuse for being indifferent to the things she saw and heard. She knew that she owed" (p. 149). As such, Tessa is caring and dedicated to genuinely helping as many people as possible. Her actions and the effects they had on the people around her haunt the novel, and though she aggravated many officials, British diplomats and business concerns (ending of course in her death), "Africans who mattered loved her to a man" (p. 32).

It is during her aid work that she becomes aware of the widespread and damaging administration of the drug Dypraxa, which kills a woman next to her in a hospital following the birth of her stillborn baby. This sets her on her investigations, with the help of the Belgian Doctor Arnold Bluhm, in an attempt to discover the truth and desperately claim justice for the corruption and indifference of European businesses and the corrupt Moi government. Tessa is so obsessive in her pursuit of the truth, and indignant about the actions of those white Europeans (like her) responsible for the suffering of many Africans, that she investigates to her death: "The great crime was more important to her than her own life" (p. 242).

SANDY WOODROW

Sandy Woodrow is the head of Chancery in Kenya for the British government, a section of the British High Commission supporting the Kenyan government in diplomatic affairs. He compares himself to a building early in the novel: "it gave off a self-sufficient, rugged impression. Woodrow, to all appearances, had the same sterling qualities" (p. 12). He is a long-standing member of the British Foreign Office, with experience in "half a dozen British overseas missions" (*ibid.*), and expects to be promoted and given a knighthood before long. After Tessa's murder, he feels guilty because of his role in suppressing her investigations by not passing on her research to the Foreign Office due to its scandalous nature, which would undermine British relationships with the corrupt Moi government in Kenya. He is doubly burdened by guilt having, despite his friendship with Justin, fallen in love with Tessa while she was alive, and even asked her unsuccessfully to elope with him. He is fully aware of the troubling nature of his role as a British foreign diplomat, due to the duplicitous nature of British businesses and government factions whose interests he must continue to protect: "Who made me what I am? England? My father? My schools? My pathetic terrified mother? Or seventeen years of lying for my country?" (p. 307).

ARNOLD BLUHM

Arnold Bluhm is a Belgian doctor of African descent who runs an organisation working in Kenya to provide medical aid and lobby pharmaceutical businesses to behave more ethically, which is "modest, it's Belgian, it's privately funded and medical" (p. 87). He is described as "the Westerner's African, bearded Apollo of the Nairobi cocktail round, charismatic, witty, beautiful" (p. 32) and "as close as you'll ever get to a *good* man" (p. 93). He too never appears alive in the novel, as he is killed along with his good friend Tessa for their collaborative investigations. Throughout the novel, it is insinuated by the press and the gossipy British diplomat community in Kenya that he and Tessa had been having an affair, and even that he killed her in the heat of passion: "your archetypal black killer. He had ensnared a white man's wife, cut her throat, decapitated her driver and run off into the bush" (p. 65). These reports prove to be wholly false, after he is revealed both to have been tortured and killed, and to have been a homosexual. Bluhm is a demonised figure in *The Constant Gardener*, reflecting the problematic representations of black people in the media, which only makes his fate and dedication all the more tragic.

ANALYSIS

HISTORICAL CONTEXT

The novel largely takes place in Nairobi, Kenya in the early 2000s, in the closing years of President Moi's tenure as president, a reign often criticised for its corruption, ineffectiveness and misuse of foreign aid. Moi was ousted as president in free elections in 2002, having been barred from running, ending over 20 years of presidency. *The Constant Gardener* also revolves around the ongoing AIDS crisis in Africa, and the way that the Moi government and a complex network of foreign diplomats and NGOs attempt to deal with the crisis. A large proportion of the world's AIDS cases at the time were diagnosed in Africa, and the poor-quality infrastructure in Kenya, corruption and inefficiency of the government, as well as the exploitative actions of Western business concerns, hugely exacerbated the situation. These events dominate the novel, as Justin follows his wife's attempts to reveal Western exploitation of African tragedy and criticism of all parties is rife. As Woodrow remembers saying to Tessa during one of their conversations:

> "The Moi government is terminally corrupt, you tell me. I never doubted it, the country is dying of AIDS, it's bankrupt, there is not a corner of it, from tourism to wildlife to education to transport to welfare to communications, that isn't falling apart from fraud, incompetence and neglect" (p. 52)

As a novel revolving around British diplomats and aid workers in Kenya, the subject of British colonialism is, of course, often referenced. At the height of the British Empire, it covered a quarter of the earth's land area, including many colonies in parts of Southern and Eastern Africa including Kenya, Sudan, Somalia and Egypt. Following the Second World War, Britain went through a sustained period of decolonisation, relinquishing many of its overseas colonies and slowly diminishing in power and influence. Kenya gained its independence in 1962, following years of uprisings and unrest, and installed its first president, Jomo Kenyatta, in 1964. Amongst the British diplomats in the novel, this dark past is often a point of reference, particularly for Tessa, who exclaims at Woodrow after he claims that the British gave Kenya independence: "We didn't bloody *give* them a thing! They *took* it! At the end of a bloody gun! We gave them nothing – nothing!" (p. 126). As we can see in the novel, Western countries are still able to exploit their former colonies through unregulated business.

CORRUPTION AND JUSTICE

The driving force of *The Constant Gardener* is Justin's exploration of Tessa's investigations into a huge corruption scandal and her attempts to seek justice for the crimes that have been committed. As such, one of its major themes, characteristic of le Carré's novels, is underlying political corruption and its monumental effects on the world. In particular, the crisis in the novel follows the disastrous effects of unethical business practices and a desperation for profit made worse by the rising power of large corporations in the world. As Kenneth K. Curtiss says: "You think countries run the fucking world? Go back to fucking Sunday school. It's "God save our multinational" they're singing these days" (p. 411). Le Carré is hugely critical in the novel of the failure of governments to police such corporations and those who profit from their activities, whose corruption runs in tandem with the exploitation of corporations in causing misery for African people. Tessa talks at one point of the fact that "Western companies, British included, were ripping off the Africans – overcharging them for technical services, dumping overpriced out-of-date medicines on them" (p. 90). Le Carré highlights the hypocrisy of foreign governments, which are in Africa on the pretext of providing assistance, but are actually making vast amounts of money from the exploitation of crisis.

Particularly in focus is the British Foreign Office in Kenya and in London, who constantly lie, cover up damning evidence and prevent the investigation from going ahead under the morally protective line of representing British business interests. Sandy Woodrow is representative of this vision of British deceit, projecting the image of British morality, level-headedness and justice to cover up major acts of collaborative corruption. Indeed, this theme is reflective of le Carré's Cold War espionage novels, such as *Tinker Tailor Soldier Spy*. He similarly focusses on corruption and duplicity within major international institutions which, just under the surface, have a massive effect on the world's geopolitical environment. This reflection shows the changing nature of the world, in which the power and malignancy of business is unregulated by governments, a place where "some pharmaceutical companies are arms dealers in shining raiment" (p. 249).

THE WHITE MAN IN AFRICA

In the early 2000s, Kenya had only been independent from the British Empire for just under 40 years. As a result, the actions of a white British 'ruling' diplomat class living in Nairobi whose lives the plot revolves around clearly echo past colonialist rule, comparisons to which reveal the hypocrisy of the moral superiority and English exceptionalism many of them show. Of a party thrown by a senior member of the Foreign Office, Woodrow reflects: "Black servants in white gloves will be hovering, just as they did in the colonial times we all piously disavow" (p. 40). Indeed, the racial and class divides between the white Europeans and local Kenyan people are stark and ubiquitous in the novel. The British diplomats live in a segregated area of wealth and comfort close to sprawling Nairobi slums in a separation of class and race that elevates them above the people they are apparently in Kenya to help. Tessa, as a conscientious and guilt-ridden member of the English upper class, is fully aware of the problematic nature of her and many of her colleague's presence in Africa, and comments:

> "A continent lies dying at our door, and here we stand or kneel drinking coffee off a silver tray while just down the road children starve, the sick die and crooked politicians bankrupt the nation that was tricked into electing them." (p. 55)

Indeed, in *The Constant Gardener* le Carré is critical not just of the British in Kenya, but of general Western influence in Africa and the way that Western business and governmental concerns use the underdeveloped nature of African infrastructure as a stomping ground for profit. He attempts to show that the idea of modernising and benevolent Western influence in the developing world is in fact largely a false one, with many of the genuine aid work in Africa being done by non-governmental organisations. The actions of the British Foreign Office in the novel are proved to be wholly unconstructive, working rather to uphold British business concern, and prop up a corrupt government. Tessa is often critical of the hypocrisy of characters like Woodrow: "You think you're solving the world's problems but actually you're the problem" (p. 114).

FURTHER REFLECTION

SOME QUESTIONS TO THINK ABOUT...

- Why is le Carré so critical of the British in Kenya in the novel?
- Many of le Carré's novels begin with the death of female characters, which psychologically haunt male protagonists. Consider this in *The Constant Gardener*. Is le Carré's representation of women a good one? Why/why not?
- What does the novel say about Britain and its decline in the world? Consider representations in the novel of British identity, and the character of 'the English gentleman'.
- Given its criticisms of world governments and global conflicts, though *The Constant Gardener* is a work of fiction, to what extent can it also be described as journalism?
- How does the novel compare to the film adaptation? Think about how you might go about adapting the book for the screen or stage.

- Think about the title of the novel. Justin Quayle is of course known for being an avid horticulturalist – but what other broader symbolic meaning might it have?
- Consider le Carré's attitudes toward Britain and its place in the world in the novel. Nearly 20 years after it was published, how has Britain's identity changed or stayed the same in the context of international relations?
- Much of the novel explores the exploitation of Africa by unethical Western concerns. Why would this have been so easy to do in Africa? Can you think of other examples of the exploitation of the developing world?
- Consider the representation of the media in *The Constant Gardener* – what do you think le Carré is trying to say about modern-day news reportage?

We want to hear from you!
Leave a comment on your online library
and share your favourite books on social media!

FURTHER READING

REFERENCE EDITION

- Le Carré, J. (2006) *The Constant Gardener.* London: Sceptre.

ADAPTATIONS

- *The Constant Gardener.* (2005) [Film]. Fernando Meirelles. Dir. USA: Focus Features.

MORE FROM BRIGHTSUMMARIES.COM

- Reading guide – *The Night Manager* by John le Carré.
- Reading guide – *Tinker Tailor Soldier Spy* by John le Carré.

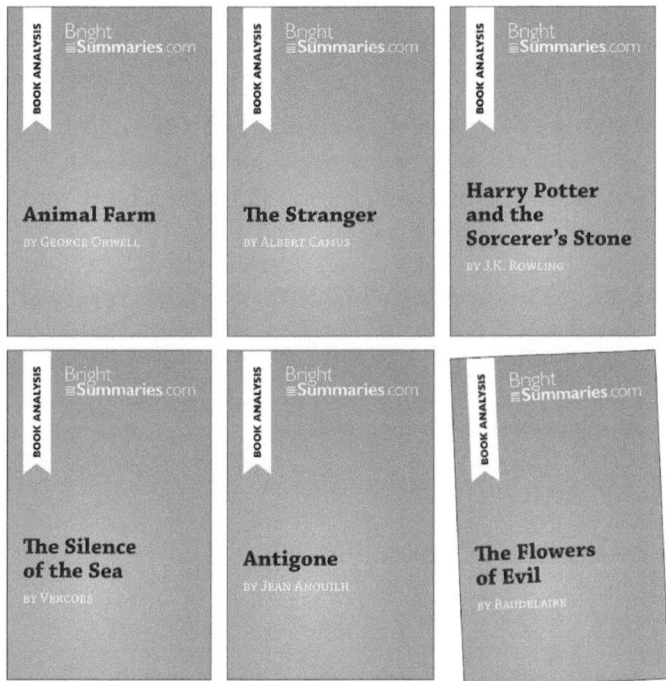

www.brightsummaries.com

Ebook EAN: 9782808016391

Paperback EAN: 9782808016407

Legal Deposit: D/2018/12603/580

Cover: © Primento

Digital conception by Primento, the digital partner of publishers.